8/04

PRIMARY SOURCES IN AMERICAN HISTORY™

SLAVERY IN AMERICA

A PRIMARY SOURCE HISTORY OF THE INTOLERABLE PRACTICE OF SLAVERY

TONYA BUELL

rosen central
Primary Source™

The Rosen Publishing Group, Inc., New York

Published in 2004 by The Rosen Publishing Group, Inc.
29 East 21st Street, New York, NY 10010

Library of Congress Cataloging-in-Publication Data

Buell, Tonya.
Slavery in America: a primary source history of the intolerable practice of slavery / by Tonya Buell. — 1st ed.
    p. cm. — (Primary sources in American history)
Summary: Uses primary source documents, narrative, and illustrations to recount the history of slavery in the United States.
Includes bibliographical references and index.
ISBN 0-8239-4513-8 (lib. bdg.)
1. Slavery—United States—History—Sources—Juvenile literature. [1. Slavery—History—Sources.]
I. Title. II. Series.
E441.B84 2004
306.3'62'0973—dc21

2003011021

Manufactured in the United States of America

On the front cover: *Slave Market*, a nineteenth-century oil painting by Eyre Crowe. From a private collection.

On the back cover: First row *(left to right)*: committee drafting the Declaration of Independence for action by the Continental Congress; Edward Braddock and troops ambushed by Indians at Fort Duquesne. Second row *(left to right)*: the *Mayflower* in Plymouth Harbor; the Oregon Trail at Barlow Cutoff. Third row *(left to right)*: slaves waiting at a slave market; the USS *Chesapeake* under fire from the HMS *Shannon*.

CONTENTS

NTRODUCTION

A Shameful Part of History

Imagine that one day, with no warning or notice whatsoever, you are kidnapped from your home and bound with chains. You are forced to march for days on end through strange lands, chained to others like a group of animals. When you reach a large sea that you've never set eyes on before, you are herded onto a ship and forced into a lower deck as dark and cold as a dungeon. For two months you live in this dungeon, cramped together with hundreds of strangers who don't even speak your language. At last, you reach a new land and are let out of the horrible prison to finally see daylight once again. But instead of being freed, you are marched onto an auction block and sold to the highest bidder.

Your new owner takes you to his home and directs you to a small one-room shack with no furniture or bedding; this will be your new home. You are made to work on a huge farm from morning until night and are given only a small amount of food and a few items of clothing. Day after day you work, and night after night you rest, as months and years go by. You have no family, and you have no hope of creating a better future for yourself. Your life is now on this farm,

Slaves in the American South were often made to work long days in the punishing sun with no breaks and little to eat. This photograph from the 1860s shows a slave family picking cotton in a field near Savannah, Georgia. It was not uncommon for a family of slaves to work together in the fields and live together in a one-room shack.

where your only belongings are a couple of pieces of clothing, a blanket, and a pot to cook your dinner in. All you have of your old life in your old land are memories, and even they are too distant for you to find much joy in. You are a slave.

This was the life of many people who came to America in the early part of the country's history. It was not the life of those immigrants who came with hopes and dreams of creating a prosperous future in a new land. Nor was it the life of those who came to escape persecution and intolerance in their old land. This was the life of those who came not of their own free will but were brought by force. This was a life without hope for a bright future, a life filled with uncertainty and misery. This was the life of slaves in America.

Slavery is a shameful part of the United States's past. The institution that allowed people to be considered little more than private property was legal and accepted by church and state alike. Some slaves, such as Harriet Tubman and Frederick Douglass, were able to rise above their stations and leave lasting legacies. But millions of others had no opportunities at all in the American system and lived and died without a chance to achieve their dreams.

TIMELINE

1619 —— Dutch merchants bring twenty Africans to the colony of Jamestown, Virginia, as indentured servants.

1739 —— The Stono Rebellion breaks out near Charleston, South Carolina.

1776 —— The United States declares its independence from Great Britain.

1793 —— The cotton gin is invented by Eli Whitney, making the production of cotton faster and easier.

1800 —— Gabriel's Rebellion is plotted in Virginia.

1808 —— Congress bans the international slave trade.

1822 —— Denmark Vesey's plot to revolt is uncovered.

1831 —— Nat Turner's rebellion breaks out near Jerusalem, Virginia.

1852 —— *Uncle Tom's Cabin*, written by Harriet Beecher Stowe, is published.

TIMELINE

1859	On October 16, John Brown leads a raid on the federal arsenal at Harpers Ferry.
1860	President Abraham Lincoln is elected.
1861	Seven Southern states secede from the Union. The Civil War starts at Fort Sumter, South Carolina.
1863	The Emancipation Proclamation ends slavery in the Confederate states.
1865	The Confederacy surrenders, ending the Civil War. The Thirteenth Amendment to the U.S. Constitution, abolishing all forms of slavery throughout the entire United States, is ratified.

# CHAPTER 1

Slavery began and later flourished in America for three main reasons. First, there was a huge need for cheap labor in early America. Second, there existed in America a belief that some people should be property owners while others should be workers. These reasons, as well as a prejudice against blacks, helped create a system that allowed room for slavery and caused early American colonists to excuse and even justify slavery. Finally, the rise of large plantations, primarily in the Southern states, and the invention of the cotton gin increased the need for good hard workers and caused the already existing tradition of slavery to flourish.

THE BEGINNINGS OF SLAVERY

Cheap Labor

When the first English colonists arrived in Jamestown, Virginia, in 1607, they began to develop the area and build towns and cities. Many of these colonists had been accustomed to hiring servants to farm their land and keep their houses, and they looked for the same type of cheap, reliable labor in the New World.

Initially, the English settlers hired white indentured servants from Europe. These servants would hire themselves out for a

When European settlers came to the New World and established Jamestown, as illustrated in the lithograph above, they found there was a lot more work to be done than they could handle themselves. Accustomed to employing servants in Europe, they continued the practice in their new home. Eventually, they hit upon the idea of buying slaves from Africa, giving them no rights and no human worth. This began the long and troubled history of race relations in the United States.

term of four to seven years in exchange for a salary and passage to the New World. This form of labor did not work for several reasons. The pay, though quite low, was too high for the colonists to afford and still make a profit on their farms. In addition, there were not enough people in Europe who were willing to come all the way to a new land and work for seven years for the small amount of money that was offered. There was a great need for farm laborers and domestic servants, yet there were very few people willing to do the job.

The settlers had to look elsewhere for labor. They considered Native Americans who already lived in America, but this source of labor did not work either. Most Native Americans did not want to work for white colonists and were willing and able to fight for their freedom. Many of those who did serve as laborers became sick and often died after being exposed to diseases, such as smallpox, brought over by the Europeans.

The settlers finally found their source for labor in blacks brought over from Europe and Africa. These men, women, and children were strong and healthy, were often immune to most of the European diseases, and were physically able to do the work that was required. The first group of these blacks to arrive in America were regarded as indentured servants, just like their white and Native American counterparts. But as time went on, blacks were given fewer and fewer rights, until eventually they became slaves with virtually no rights at all.

Prejudicial Beliefs

The Europeans who settled the American colonies in the seventeenth and eighteenth centuries didn't regard slavery as inhumane or evil. They generally considered blacks to be subhuman, so giving them no rights was not immoral in their eyes.

Because African culture was so different from European culture, many early settlers thought of Africans as uncivilized savages. The few blacks that they had seen in Europe were servants or

The United States Constitution is the oldest written constitution of a major nation and has served as a model for the constitutions of many countries around the world. Although the United States was founded on, among other things, the principles of equality and liberty, the Constitution did not specifically address the freedom of slaves or blacks in general. In fact, since slaves were considered property, and since even free blacks were not widely seen as members of society, they were not included in the rights articulated in the Constitution. See transcription excerpt on page 55.

12

slaves. It seemed natural for them to use Africans as slaves to help them succeed in the New World.

When the first blacks were brought from Africa, in 1619, they were regarded as indentured servants, with the same rights and status as the white indentured servants who lived in America. Eventually, however, due to the colonists' racial prejudices, black servants lost these rights, while the white servants retained them. When courts ruled against servants who had broken the law, white servants had their servitude extended, while black servants became servants for life. Finally, blacks became slaves with virtually no rights under the law.

The colonies' early legal systems even allowed for slavery. The Body of Liberties, a group of laws enacted in 1641 in Massachusetts, outlawed slavery except in certain circumstances. Slavery was not illegal altogether; it was allowed in various situations. Other colonies enacted similar laws, expanding the circumstances under which slavery could be allowed. In effect, slavery was legal. The European custom of keeping Africans as slaves continued when America's government was created.

The U.S. Constitution, widely equated with the notions of freedom and justice, even allowed for slavery in a few of its articles. In Article I, for example, the Constitution states that "representatives and direct taxes shall be apportioned . . . according to . . . [the] number of free persons . . . [and] three-fifths of all other persons." This assumes the existence of people who are not free. Article IV deals with fugitive slaves, stating that any person "held to service or labor in one State" who escapes into another presumably free state shall not automatically be free.

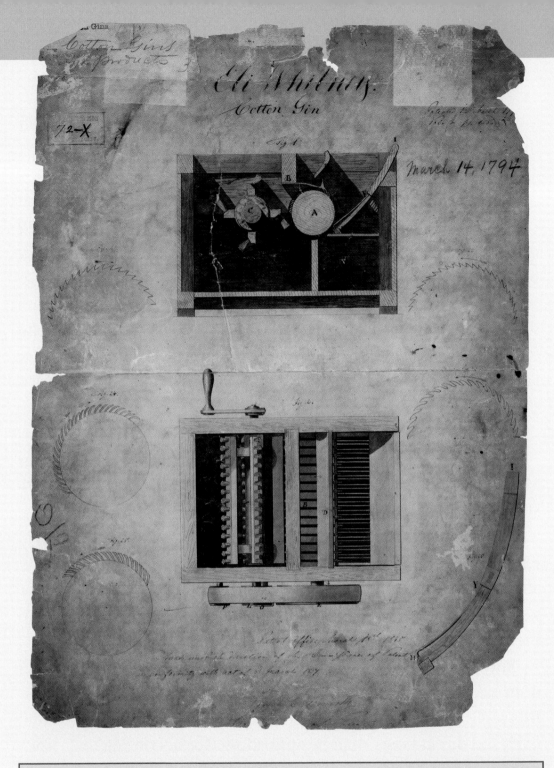

Although machines that removed the seeds from cotton fiber had been around for a long time, Eli Whitney's cotton gin of 1793 was the first to clean short-staple cotton. Whitney's 1794 patent is shown above. With his invention, 50 pounds (22.7 kilograms) of cotton could be cleaned in a day. For the first time, cotton was a crop that brought profits. In time, the United States produced three-quarters of the world's cotton supply, and cotton was the largest American export.

It wasn't until after the Civil War that the Constitution finally outlawed all forms of slavery in the United States.

Large Plantations

In the early American colonies, there was an abundance of land and very few people. The amount of crops that a person could grow on that land, therefore, depended on how many people he or she could get to work on it. Labor was in high demand.

Initially, tobacco, rice, and sugar were grown on big farms in the American colonies. In 1793, a man named Eli Whitney was credited with inventing the cotton gin, a machine that made it possible for cotton to be processed much faster than before. There was a great demand for cotton in Europe at the time, and there were large amounts of empty land in the American South on which it could be grown. Therefore, large cotton planta-tions sprang up, and the need for suitable labor rose higher than ever before.

As the cotton crop grew, the number of slaves in the United States grew with it. Greedy landowners paid good money for slaves who could work on their farms all of their lives. Between 1790 and 1810, the number of slaves in the United States more than tripled. Slavery, at least in the Southern colonies, became recognized as an institution that was not only useful but necessary.

CHAPTER 2

Most of the people who were brought to the United States during the slave trade of the seventeenth, eighteenth, and nineteenth centuries came from West Africa. They usually lived in small villages composed of several extended families, and they often had farms, where they grew crops such as yams and grains and herded cattle and other livestock. Some villages specialized in metalwork, pottery, or woodcarving, trading their goods at local markets for food, clothing, and other necessities.

THE SLAVE TRADE

Europeans initially traveled to Africa in search of gold and other treasures. After the demand for slaves in America skyrocketed, many went to Africa in search of slaves. Slave traders created wars between villages and took advantage of the fighting by purchasing Africans who had been captured by their enemies. They also persuaded Africans to kidnap people from enemy villages to sell as slaves.

After being captured or purchased, African slaves were forced to march, shackled and chained together, as far as 1,000 miles to coastal trading posts, where they were held in underground dungeons or prisons until they boarded slave ships. According to PBS.org, only half of the people who started this grueling march survived it. Those who did survive had no idea of the horror that was to come.

Once they were captured, African slaves were chained together and marched hundreds of miles to the coast, where they would board ships and eventually sail to America. Slave traders became rich from the purchase of these prisoners, but they were not the only ones who benefited. Working with slave traders and enjoying a cut of the profits were the slaves' fellow Africans, whose job it was to kidnap their countrymen and transport them to the traders.

The Middle Passage

The trip to America on a slave ship was extremely harsh. It usually took two to four months. Food was scarce, and space was even scarcer. Slave traders packed their ships with 300 to 400 slaves, all stuffed in spaces too low to stand up. Slaves were chained together from wrist to wrist or ankle to ankle, and they were forced to lie on their backs for hours or days at a time in a space the size of a coffin.

Death of Capt. Ferrer, the Captain of the Amistad, July, 1839.

Don Jose Ruiz and Don Pedro Montez, of the Island of Cuba, having purchased fifty-three slaves at Havana, recently imported from Africa, put them on board the Amistad, Capt. Ferrer, in order to transport them to Principe, another port on the Island of Cuba. After being out from Havana about four days, the African captives on board, in order to obtain their freedom, and return to Africa, armed themselves with cane knives, and rose upon the Captain and crew of the vessel. Capt. Ferrer and the cook of the vessel were killed; two of the crew escaped; Ruiz and Montez were made prisoners.

Published in 1840, the illustration above depicts the slave revolt on board the *Amistad* in 1839. The caption below the illustration tells the story: "Death of Capt. Ferrer, the Captain of the Amistad, July, 1839. Don Jose Ruiz and Don Pedro Montez, of the Island of Cuba, having purchased fifty-three slaves at Havana, recently imported from Africa, put them on board the Amistad, Capt. Ferrer, in order to transport them to Principe, another port on the Island of Cuba. After being out from Havana about four days, the African captives on board, in order to obtain their freedom, and return to Africa, armed themselves with cane knives, and rose upon the Captain and crew of the vessel. Capt. Ferrer and the cook of the vessel were killed; two of the crew escaped; Ruiz and Montez were made prisoners."

Many got sick and died. There were very few washing facilities for the slaves on the ships, and they often had to lie in their own and others' vomit, excrement, and blood. Diseases like smallpox, yellow fever, and dysentery spread like wildfire in the close quarters. Since crew members of the ships couldn't bear the awful stench that surrounded the miserable slaves, they seldom cleaned the ships or removed dead bodies. Slaves were forced to lie side by side with the dead for days or even weeks at a time. Many slaves went mad, and some jumped overboard to avoid facing more of the horrors that they had already seen.

Some slave ship captains even forced sick slaves to jump overboard and drown, so that they would not contaminate the

This illustration of the stowage of the British slave ship the *Brookes* shows how overcrowded slaves' quarters were when slaves journeyed across the Atlantic to the United States. According to the Regulated Slave Trade Act of 1788, the maximum slave capacity on the *Brookes* was set at 454. The *Brookes*, tightly packed with as many slaves as could fit, illegally carried closer to 609 (351 men, 127 women, 90 boys, and 41 girls).

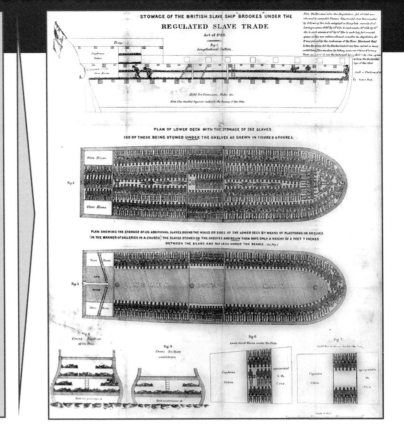

healthy slaves on the ship. On one slave ship, 132 sick slaves were forced overboard so that the ship's captain would be able to collect money from the insurance company. Insurance paid for dead slaves but not for sick ones.

Olaudah Equiano

Olaudah Equiano was born to a prosperous family in West Africa in about 1745. He was kidnapped by slave traders as a child and was sent to live as a slave in America. Gustavus Vassa was the name given to him by his owners. Equiano learned to read and write, and in 1766, he purchased his freedom. In his autobiography, *The Interesting Narrative of the Life of Olaudah Equiano, or Gustavus Vassa, the African*, he describes his capture and transport to America:

One day, when all our people were gone out to their works as usual and only I and my dear sister were left to

As if it wasn't dehumanizing enough to be kidnapped, shackled, marched, starved, and crammed onto an overcrowded ship, slaves often died or were killed after having endured so much. Slave traders regularly threw ill slaves overboard, since they no longer had value to the trader and might infect the rest of the captives. Sometimes, traders rid their ships of a few slaves so that they wouldn't get fined for carrying more than was legal or so they could collect insurance money.

mind the house, two men and a woman got over our walls, and in a moment seized us both, and without giving us time to cry out or make resistance they stopped our mouths and ran off with us into the nearest wood . . . [I was taken] through different countries and various nations, till at the end of six or seven months after I had been kidnapped I arrived at the sea coast.

Equiano described the ship:

[It] was so crowded that each had scarcely room to turn himself, [and it] almost suffocated us . . . The air became unfit for respiration from a variety of loathsome smells, and brought on a sickness among the slaves, of which many died . . . This wretched situation was again aggravated by the galling of the chains . . . and the filth of the necessary tubs, into which the children often fell and were almost suffocated.

One day, when we had a smooth sea and moderate wind, two of my wearied countrymen who were chained together (I was near them at the time), preferring death to such a life of misery, somehow made through the nettings and jumped into the sea.

The Auction Block

Once slave ships reached America, the slaves were sold at auctions. Slave ship captains would prepare their human cargo for the auction to make them look young and healthy. The healthier the slaves looked, the more money the trader could fetch. Slaves were fed fattening foods and cleaned and oiled. Any gray hairs were plucked or dyed. Tar was smeared over open wounds to hide them.

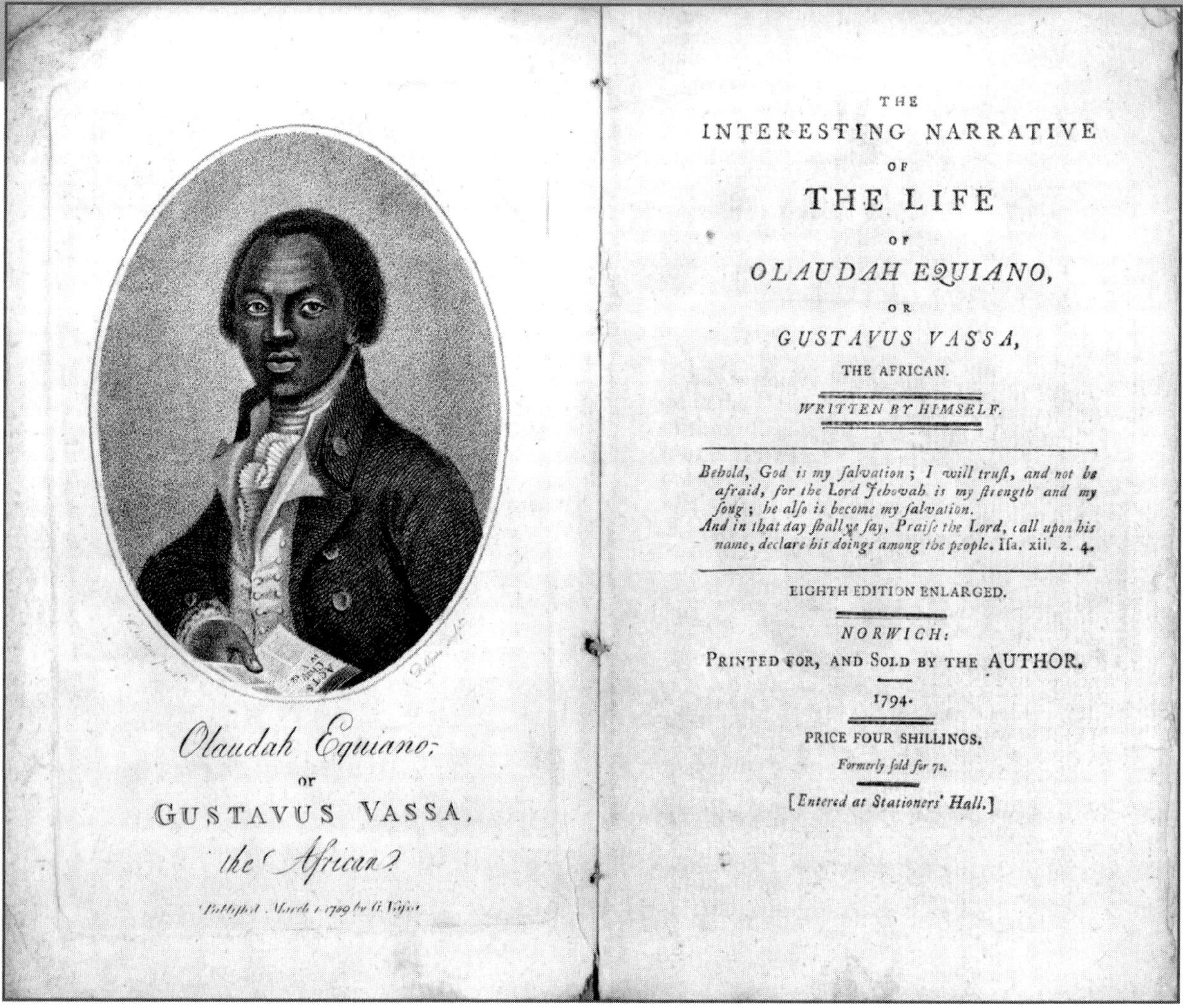

THE
INTERESTING NARRATIVE
OF
THE LIFE
OF
OLAUDAH EQUIANO,
OR
GUSTAVUS VASSA,
THE AFRICAN.

WRITTEN BY HIMSELF.

Behold, God is my salvation; I will trust, and not be
afraid, for the Lord Jehovah is my strength and my
song; he also is become my salvation.
And in that day shall ye say, Praise the Lord, call upon his
name, declare his doings among the people. Isa. xii. 2. 4.

EIGHTH EDITION ENLARGED.

NORWICH:
PRINTED FOR, AND SOLD BY THE AUTHOR.
1794.

PRICE FOUR SHILLINGS.
Formerly sold for 7s.

[Entered at Stationers' Hall.]

Olaudah Equiano;
or
GUSTAVUS VASSA,
the African?

Published March 1 1789 by G. Vassa

Former slave Olaudah Equiano, also known as Gustavus Vassa, wrote his auto-biography (the frontispiece is shown above) and registered it in London in 1789. The book became a worldwide best seller and is still recognized as one of the first works written in English by a former slave. Books like Equiano's informed the public of the horrors of slavery and also started the switch from an oral tradition to a written one among African Americans.

At the auction, potential buyers inspected the slaves that had arrived. Slaves were poked and prodded, and their teeth and muscles were inspected to determine how healthy they were and how much work they would be able to do. Sometimes they were forced to prance or jump to show their agility.

This print from *Harper's Weekly* shows a slave auction in the South. During these episodes of humiliation, slaves were poked and prodded like animals and were often separated from their families and friends. The largest slave auction to occur in the United States was held by plantation owner Pierce M. Butler in 1859. Massively in debt, Butler was forced to sell his slaves in an auction known as the Weeping Time. Four hundred thirty-six men, women, and children who had grown together as a family were sold and scattered around the South.

Slaves were then sold to the highest bidder. It didn't matter if one had family or friends. Mothers were separated from their children, siblings were split up, and wives were taken from their husbands. These sorrows and humiliations would continue throughout much of their lives in America.

CHAPTER 3

Whe slaves were purchased by white landowners, they began a life of hardship and toil. They learned to follow directions or else be harshly punished, and they learned that they must get along with one another as best they could.

Slaves worked very hard to keep the plantations, households, and businesses that they worked for running smoothly. Slaves had a broad range of occupations, ranging from farm laborers and household servants to skilled laborers and craftsmen. Some slave owners leased their slaves out to other farmers, landowners, or business owners.

THE LIVES OF SLAVES

The majority of slaves worked from sunup to sundown in the fields of large plantations. They tended crops and harvested them when they were grown. They worked under the close supervision of white overseers, who punished them for the slightest misdeeds, and black drivers, who forced them to work harder and faster. On some plantations, the overseers assigned a task in the morning. When it was complete, the slaves attended to their own gardens and other needs.

Household slaves worked as domestic servants, cooking, cleaning, and tending and nursing the children. Female slaves nursed the babies, cared for the children, cleaned the house, and cooked the meals. Male slaves built and repaired the houses,

The WASHINGTON FAMILY.   La FAMILLE de WASHINGTON.

George Washington his Lady and her two Grandchildren by the name of Custis.   George Washington Son Épouse et Ses deux petits Enfants du Nom de

In this portrait of George Washington's family, painted by American painter Edward Savage, Washington is shown posing with his wife, her grandchildren, and a black house servant. (Washington had forty-one servants.) Domestic, or household, slaves had many advantages over their field counterparts. Because they were considered to have more value than field slaves, they were often treated relatively better by their masters and were less likely to be severely beaten or sold to another plantation. Household slaves dressed better, were fed better, and moved about with greater freedom. They were also in a position to become closer to their masters and to know them more intimately.

tended the livestock, and drove the carriages. All slaves worked very hard, often every day of the week, to keep things in the household running smoothly.

Family

Families were an important part of slave life, but they were also a source of much sadness. Most slave women had children, but unfortunately many children were sold off to different masters, never to see their families again. A mother, father, daughter, or son could be sold at any time, and on numerous occasions the entire family was separated. Slaves tried to obey their masters and work very hard so that they would not be sold to another master, but if the master needed money, the slave might still be sold.

Many slave masters sexually abused and impregnated their female slaves. The laws stated that children of female slaves would also be slaves, so even though these children had white— and often wealthy—fathers, they remained slaves.

Since slaves could be sold at any time, they were never given the legal right to marry. However, they developed their own traditions and customs and "married" anyway. When a young man and woman wanted to marry, they went to an elder in their community, who prepared a ceremony. All of the community's slaves gathered together and prayed for the marriage. A broom was placed across the doorway of the cabin where the couple planned to live. The couple held hands and jumped over the broom, thus becoming man and wife.

Living Conditions

Slaves' living conditions were harsh, and sometimes slaves got sick or died simply for lack of food or shelter. Slave owners

This famous painting by an unknown artist depicts a slave wedding in the early nineteenth century. The fact that slave marriages were not legal because slaves were considered property of their masters didn't keep slaves from marrying one another. Most took their vows very seriously and remained married until death. Weddings ran the gamut from simple broomstick ceremonies like the one shown above to elaborate ceremonies and celebrations planned by the master's wife.

wanted their slaves to survive because they were valuable property, but they also did not want to spend money keeping their slaves healthy. Slaves were often left to fend for themselves, preparing their own meals and catching oysters or fish to live on, usually after a long day of work on the plantation.

Some slaves, especially domestic or household slaves, were able to eat leftovers from their masters' meals. Plantation workers, who worked from morning until night in the fields, were given a ration of food once a week or once a month, and they

Slaves from a Georgia plantation stand outside their quarters in this photograph from the mid-1800s. Although field slaves generally were exposed to harsher working conditions than domestic slaves, they did have more independence in their living quarters. After a long day's work in the field, they could return to their quarters and communicate freely. This meant that they could pass on their beliefs and oral traditions to their families.

were expected to cook their own meals after their day's work was done. They were given a quantity of cornmeal and some meat, which they sometimes supplemented with food from their garden or fish from a nearby river. Since they had very little time to cook their food, they made hoecakes out of cornmeal batter by cooking them on a hot hoe while working out in the fields.

Slaves lived in log cabins that were set in rows far from the big, beautiful plantation mansion. They often lived in close quarters, with an entire family or several people living in a small one-room cabin. The bed was often just a crude mattress laid on the floor, and the furniture was scarce. Some slaves had gardens, but they could tend these gardens only after their day's work was done, and they were frequently very tired.

First-Person Accounts of Slavery

Frederick Douglass was a slave who secretly taught himself to read and write and eventually became a great leader among his people. His autobiography, *Narrative of the Life of Frederick Douglass, an American Slave*, describes the living conditions of slaves in great detail.

In one section of his autobiography, he described the separation of families.

My mother and I were separated when I was but an infant—before I knew her as my mother. It is a common custom, in the part of Maryland from which I ran away, to part children from their mothers at a very early age. Frequently, before the child has reached its twelfth month, its mother is taken from it, and hired out on some farm a considerable distance off, and the child is placed under the care of an old woman, too old for field labor.

He also wrote about some of the basic living conditions.

Here, too, the slaves of all the other farms received their monthly allowance of food, and their yearly clothing. The men and women slaves received, as their monthly allowance of food, eight pounds of pork, or its equivalent in fish, and one bushel of corn meal. Their yearly

clothing consisted of two coarse linen shirts, one pair of linen trousers, like the shirts, one jacket, one pair of trousers for winter, made of coarse Negro cloth, one pair of stockings, and one pair of shoes . . . There were no beds given the slaves, unless one coarse blanket be considered such, and none but the men and women had these . . . [They were very tired, because] when their day's work in the field is done, the most of them having their washing, mending, and cooking to do . . . when this is done, old and young, male and female, married and single, drop down side by side, on one common bed,— the cold, damp floor,—each covering himself or herself with their miserable blankets; and here they sleep till they are summoned to the field by the driver's horn.

Fanny Kemble was a white actress who married a wealthy plantation owner named Pierce Butler. Although she was ambiva-

Painted by Henry Inman in the nineteenth century, this oil portrait shows the English actress Fanny Kemble Butler. Kemble was an accomplished writer, speaker, and athlete. Her strongest trait was her independence. She fell in love with an heir named Pierce Butler without knowing the source of his wealth. (He was the plantation owner whose massive sale of slaves was called the Weeping Time.) Shocked at the slaves' conditions at his plantation, Kemble eventually left Butler.

lent about slavery at first, she became a staunch abolitionist when she saw the horrible way slaves lived. This is an excerpt from her journal.

I beg you to bear in mind that the Negroes on Mr. [Butler]'s estate are generally considered well off. They go to the fields at daybreak, carrying with them their allowance of food for the day, which toward noon, and not till then, they eat, cooking it over a fire, which they kindle as best they can, where they are working. Their second meal in the day is at night, after their labor is over, having worked, at the very least, six hours without intermission of rest or refreshment since their noonday meal.

Kemble published her journal to dissuade England from supporting the Confederacy. But literature describing the horrors of slavery helped the abolitionist cause gain support.

CHAPTER 4

Although many slaves accepted their existence, living peacefully according to the laws of their owners, many others refused to. Faced with a lifetime of suffering under unfair laws and living in harsh conditions, many slaves decided to fight back.

Resistance to slavery took many different forms. Some slaves resisted in simple ways like doing their work incorrectly or breaking tools. Many attempted escape. Some used the Underground Railroad, a set of safe places where escaped slaves could go to hide, to ensure their safe passage to the North. There were also slave revolts, in which a group of slaves banded together to fight their white masters and take back their freedom.

Everyday Resistance

In order to get out of doing certain, more difficult tasks, slaves often pretended to be confused or stupid. They would go to the wrong place, bring the wrong tools, and pretend to never quite

When slaves dared to escape from their masters, notices were posted around the area for their return. One such broadside is shown at right. Even if a slave made it to freedom, he or she always had to worry about being turned in by someone who might want the reward offered by the slave's master.

$200 REWARD.

RAN AWAY from the Subscriber, on the 21st of October, his Negro Man, called **WARNER SALE**. He is about 35 years of age, copper-colored, about 5 feet 10 inches high, well made, stout built, bow-legged, a small piece broken out of one of his front teeth, a small scar on the lid of one of his eyes, small moustache and goatee, is polite when spoken to, and is fond of drinking. Clothing not recollected, but has a good supply with him. I will give the above reward for his apprehension and return to me, or if lodged in any jail, so that I get him again.

R. P. WARING,
Loretto Post Office, Essex Co., Va.

Nov. 2, 1853.

33

understand how to do the work that was required. This type of resistance could prove quite costly to the slave owner, especially when slaves broke expensive tools or damaged valuable crops, or when they left gates open and let the slaveholder's valuable livestock wander away. Slaves were not really confused or stupid, of course, but they pretended to be so in order to deceive and inconvenience their cruel masters.

Some slaves would pretend to be sick to get out of doing certain work. They usually got away with it, since smart slave owners recognized them as expensive assets and wanted them to get healthy. Female slaves even pretended to be pregnant so that they would have less work to do and get more food to eat.

Sometimes the everyday resistances turned into something more severe. Instead of just cooking the food improperly, a slave might "accidentally" poison the master's food, causing the master and his or her family to get sick and possibly even die. Untended fires "accidentally" burnt down barns, crops, and even the mansions that the slave owners lived in. Some slaves even killed themselves, preferring death to a life of bondage.

Escape

Many slaves tried to escape to the North or to Canada, where they would be free. Although there were numerous difficulties with escaping, many slaves tried anyway, and quite a few made it. The slaves who escaped had a number of challenges to face. First, they had no money and were able to bring with them little or no food and water. They had to beg for food from people who they hoped would be sympathetic to their plight. Unfortunately, they had no idea whom to trust: Even poor whites or free blacks might capture them and turn them in to receive a reward.

This is a slave pass from 1845. It was issued to a slave named Alfred in Virginia. The pass allowed Alfred to travel in and around Washington, D.C. Without written permission, slaves were not permitted to leave their owners' plantations. See transcription on pages 55–56.

In addition, their former master, as well as many ruthless slave hunters with dogs, would be searching for them, and they had to find good hiding places.

Still, many slaves escaped successfully and reached freedom. They dreamed up ingenious plots to fool their masters and the slave hunters who searched for them. Slaves who could write wrote passes for themselves or their family or friends. A pass stating that the slave was free to travel throughout the countryside was enough to avoid being taken by slave hunters. Slaves who were of mixed race and light in color could dress in their masters' clothing and try to pass as white. Some slaves who were light in color escaped with a friend, one pretending to be the master and the other acting as his or her slave. Before the Fugitive

THE

ANTI-SLAVERY RECORD.

VOL. I.   **MAY, 1835.**   **NO. 5.**

This engraving, titled *Cruelties of Slavery*, appeared as an illustration in *The Anti-Slavery Record* of May 1835. Slaveholders had various methods of punishing their slaves, some of them creative, all of them cruel. Disobedient or unproductive slaves were whipped, burned, branded, and "smoked" in tobacco smokehouses. As slave Harriet Jacobs wrote in *Incidents in the Life of a Slave Girl* (1861), "A favorite [punishment] was to tie a rope round a man's body, and suspend him from the ground. A fire was kindled over him, from which was suspended a piece of fat pork. As this cooked, the scalding drops of fat continually fell on the bare flesh."

Slave Laws, which stated that slave hunters could search for and return slaves even in the free states, slaves near a free state could simply run across the border and seek refuge with abolitionists or free blacks.

Escaping from a life of bondage to freedom, often which was just over the state line, was incredibly tempting. To counter the temptation and attempt to stop slaves from running away, stiff punishments were given to those who attempted escape. Slave hunters were given large rewards for catching escaped slaves. Here are some of the rewards posted on runaway notices in the South:

- "Reward of twenty shillings"

- "$50 paid to whomever returns him"

- "Wanted dead—with his head separated from his body"

The punishment for attempting to escape was very severe. Slaveholders wanted to discourage their slaves from attempting to escape, so if an escaped slave was caught, the slaveholder would exact very strict punishments to make an example of that person. The punishment for trying to escape varied widely depending on the master and could range from a severe whipping to dismemberment or even death. Many slaves who attempted to escape were sold to other masters far away, so that slave would most likely never see his or her family and friends again. Escape was a difficult way to resist, but if it was accomplished, the freedom gained was well worth the difficulties.

The Underground Railroad

The Underground Railroad was neither underground nor a railroad but instead was a secret way to help escaped slaves find their way to freedom. The Underground Railroad used many railroad terms to

Fugitive slaves escape from Maryland in this 1872 wood engraving. The Underground Railroad helped more than 100,000 slaves escape from the South. Fleeing the confines of slavery was risky business but so was assisting a fugitive slave. Those who did faced arrest, fines, and social punishment from their community.

define different parts of the trip. A "station" was any place where escaped slaves could safely stop to eat and rest. A station could be a safe house, a Quaker village, or even a barn. The "conductor" was the person who led escaped slaves out of the South to freedom in the North. People who ran the stations or who let slaves use their homes or barns to hide from slave hunters while they rested were called "station masters." These people provided food, shelter, clothes, and money to help slaves along their way.

The most famous conductor on the Underground Railroad was Harriet Tubman. Harriet Tubman was born a slave, but she escaped by traveling ninety miles from Maryland to Pennsylvania. After she became free, she made nineteen journeys back to the South and led approximately 300 slaves to freedom. She and the slaves whom she helped used secret passwords and traveled in disguise, usually traveling by night between safe houses or stations. She was hated by slave owners, and despite having a price of $40,000 (more than $500,000 U.S. today) on her head, she was never caught.

Revolts

Sometimes, slaves would get a band of other slaves together and plan an uprising. The group would gather weapons and fight their white masters for their freedom. No slave revolt was successful, but all of them worried white slave owners tremendously.

In 1739, an African man named Jemmy led a march of rebellious slaves from Stono, South Carolina, toward Florida, in hopes of reaching Mexico. Many slaves joined in their march, which grew to almost 100 people. The group, which became known as the Stono Rebellion, killed dozens of white people on its way. Finally, white colonists caught up with them, captured as many as they could, and executed them.

In 1800, a slave named Gabriel, who was a skilled blacksmith, started making swords and bullets out of metal. He recruited many other slaves throughout the state of Virginia, and they planned to attack their white slave owners on the night of August 30, 1800. Unfortunately for them, it rained heavily that night and they had to postpone their attack to a later date. Before they could actually carry out the attack, their plot was discovered. The slaves who had plotted the rebellion were arrested and sent to trial, and Gabriel and twenty-five other slaves were executed.

Nearly twenty years later, a slave name Denmark Vesey spent four years carefully planning a revolt. Unfortunately, his plans were betrayed in May 1822, and thirty-five of the conspirators were executed, while forty-two others were deported, forced to leave their families and life as they knew it, to become slaves in another land.

Finally, in 1831, a slave named Nat Turner planned a rebellion. Nat Turner had been seeing religious visions for many years, and he believed that God wanted him to attack his white oppressors. One night in August 1831, Nat Turner and seven other slaves began killing white men, women, and children. The rebellion grew to more than forty men, and at least fifty-seven white people were brutally murdered. State and federal troops were sent out to stop the revolt, and more than fifty rebels were caught. The rebels were brought to trial, along with Nat Turner, who was found guilty, hanged, and then skinned. Angry white mobs killed over 200 innocent slaves after the rebellion because they were afraid more revolts were being planned.

# CHAPTER 5

Although slavery came to be very widespread in the United States, especially in the South, and although it was an important part of the United States's economy, not everyone believed that black people should be slaves. Many people realized that slavery was cruel and inhumane, and they wanted to stop it altogether. These people were called abolitionists. To abolish something is to stop it. Abolitionists wanted to stop slavery.

There were many abolitionists throughout the United States, but the main groups were the free blacks, the Quakers, the revolutionaries, and, later, many people in the free Northern states.

Free Blacks

The free blacks who lived in the United States during the time of slavery believed that enslavement of their fellow black people was wrong. They knew that they were not inferior to whites and that they did not deserve to be enslaved. Many free blacks were former slaves who had been freed by their masters or who had managed to escape, and therefore they had seen firsthand the horrors that slavery brought to their people.

The free black community created numerous organizations to help others and to fight for the abolition of slavery. In 1787,

Absalom Jones, one of the founders of the Free African Society, is portrayed in this 1810 painting by Raphaelle Peale. Jones (1746–1818) and cofounder Richard Allen (1760–1831) were both slaves who purchased their freedom. They were instrumental in gaining religious freedom for blacks. With other free blacks, the two established the Free African Society in 1787 "to support one another in sickness, and for the benefit of their widows and fatherless children."

the Free African Society was created by two free black men, Absalom Jones and Richard Allen. This society was originally created to help widows and the poor, but it was eventually expanded to fight slavery. In Philadelphia in 1830, the American Society of Free Persons of Colour was born. It was created to help members of the black community and to fight for the abolition of slavery.

These organizations performed a number of functions in the fight against slavery. They helped runaway slaves who were on their way farther north or to Canada. They assisted blacks who had been slaves in getting jobs and homes. They urged Congress to repeal the Fugitive Slave Laws, which stated that escaped slaves could be recaptured and returned to their masters, and they asked Congress for the emancipation, or freedom, of all black people.

Quakers

The Quakers were another group who fought for the abolition of slavery. The Quakers were a religious group who believed that all people should be treated with kindness and compassion. Unlike slave traders, Quakers believed that blacks and whites should both be treated fairly.

In 1688, a proclamation protesting slavery entitled the Germantown Protest was published by a group of Quakers. It stated, "[T]ho they are black, we cannot conceive there is more liberty to have them as slaves, as it is to have other white ones ... And those who steal or robb men, and those who buy or purchase them, are they not all alike?"

Quakers who lived in the Southern states refused to own slaves, and many boycotted slave-produced goods. In 1759, the Quakers decided to disown any member who was involved in buying or selling slaves, and in 1772, they officially condemned the slave trade by a unanimous vote.

Revolutionaries

The revolutionaries who fought for America's independence from Great Britain risked their lives to gain freedom for everyone in the United States. Yet many revolutionaries were slaveholders. It didn't make sense to grant "life, liberty and the pursuit of happiness" to only a choice few, leaving out

OBSERVATIONS

On the Inslaving, importing and purchasing of

Negroes;

With some Advice thereon, extracted from the Epistle of the Yearly-Meeting of the People called QUAKERS, held at *London* in the Year 1748.

Anthony Benezet

When ye spread forth your Hands, I will hide mine Eyes from you, yea when ye make many Prayers I will not hear; your Hands are full of Blood. Wash ye, make you clean, put away the Evil of your Doings from before mine Eyes Isai. 1, 15.

Is not this the Feast that I have chosen, to loose the Bands of Wickedness, to undo the heavy Burden, to let the Oppressed go free, and that ye break every Toke, Chap. 58, 7.

Second Edition.

GERMANTOWN:
Printed by CHRISTOPHER SOWER. 1760.

Anthony Benezet's "Observations On the Inslaving, importing and purchasing of Negroes" was presented at the yearly meeting of Quakers in London, England. Quakers were among the most staunch abolitionists, and they played a great part in organizing and running the Underground Railroad, even when aiding slaves became a criminal act. Some groups of Quakers refused to use anything that had been produced as a result of slavery. For instance, to boycott white sugar that came from plantations using slave labor, Quakers would use maple sugar in their coffee. Not all Quakers believed in vocalizing their beliefs: For every Quaker who spoke out against the institution, there were many who refused to mix with the outside world and simply prayed that God would bring an end to the practice. See transcription on page 56.

thousands of black slaves, many of whom had fought for the revolutionary cause.

This double standard led many people to think twice about slavery. As John Allen, a prominent white colonist, stated in the newspaper *The Watchman's Alarm*, "What is a trifling three-penny duty on tea [referring to taxation by the British] compared to inestimable blessings of liberty to one captive?" Many slaveholders who had fought so hard for their own freedom realized that it was hypocritical to hold others in bondage, and they freed their slaves or provided a will that ensured their slaves freedom upon their death.

Uncle Tom's Cabin

Harriet Beecher Stowe was an ardent abolitionist who used her talent for writing to further the abolitionist movement. In her novel *Uncle Tom's Cabin*, she described the horrors that slaves confronted every day.

Tell me that any man living wants to work all his days, from day-dawn till dark, under the constant eye of a master, without the power of putting forth one irresponsible volition, on the same dreary, monotonous, unchanging toil, and all for two pairs of pantaloons and a pair of shoes a year, with enough food and shelter to keep him in working order! . . . I'll say, besides, that ours is the more bold and palpable infringement of human rights; actually buying a man up, like a horse,—looking at his teeth, cracking his joints, and trying his paces, and then paying down for him,—having speculators, breeders, traders, and brokers in human bodies and souls.

Uncle Tom's Cabin was such an eye-opener to the American public that it is considered to have helped bring about the Civil War. The poster shown here advertises the novel as "The Greatest Book of the Age." Although the novel was generally well received, many critics remained skeptical of its truths. An 1852 review in the *Boston Post* read, "In a word, the effect of Uncle Tom's Cabin, as a whole, is grossly to exaggerate the actual evils of negro slavery in this country . . . [I]t should be swallowed with a considerable dose of allowance."

Northern States

As time went on, more and more people became aware of the horrors of slavery and decided to join the abolitionist movement. Freed and escaped slaves in the North spread their stories through writing and speeches at antislavery meetings, convincing many Northerners that the slave trade was cruel and wrong. Books such as *Narrative of the Life of Frederick Douglass, an American Slave, Uncle Tom's Cabin*, and Fanny Kemble's *Journal of a Residence on a Georgia Plantation* added fuel to the fire. As whites in the North grew to understand the plight of their black brethren in the South, they began to realize that slavery was very wrong. Many attended antislavery meetings and boycotted goods produced by slaves.

The abolitionist John Brown (1800–1859) believed that slavery was a sin against Christianity. He worked hard to abolish it and used his house to hide runaway slaves. In time, he began to think that force was the only solution. His famous stand-off at Harpers Ferry, West Virginia, resulted in his death (convicted of treason, murder, and inciting slaves to rebellion, Brown was hanged on December 2, 1859), but his message lived on. His actions attracted attention from Northerners and Southerners alike and, like *Uncle Tom's Cabin*, may have been partially responsible for starting the Civil War.

Others organized fairs and rallies to promote the antislavery movement and to urge politicians to fight against slavery.

As the United States added more territories to the West, there were bitter disagreements about whether slavery should exist in these new territories. This led to bitter and sometimes bloody clashes, like the one at Harpers Ferry, West Virginia, where John Brown, a militant abolitionist, raided the federal arsenal of weapons in an effort to arm slaves so that they could revolt. Although he was unsuccessful, many people began more and more to understand the wickedness of slavery.

CHAPTER 6

When Abraham Lincoln was elected president of the United States in 1860, the white slaveholders in the South knew that he believed slavery was unjust. They feared that he might attempt to outlaw it. To counter this, they voted to secede, or withdraw, from the Union (the United States) so that they would be able to make their own laws and not be under the legal code of the United States government.

THE END OF SLAVERY

By February 1, 1861, only three months after Lincoln was elected, seven states— South Carolina, Alabama, Mississippi, Florida, Georgia, Louisiana, and Texas— had all voted to withdraw from the Union. Although eight other states— Missouri, Kentucky, Arkansas, Virginia, Delaware, Maryland, Tennessee, and North Carolina—were slave states, they chose to remain with the Union for the time being.

The seven states that seceded created a new government, the Confederate States of America. They believed that each state should make its own laws instead of being subjected to the laws made by a federal government, and since many of the voters in these states were slave owners, they knew that they would not abolish slavery on their own. They chose Jefferson Davis to be the president of this new confederacy.

The raising of the first flag of independence in the South is depicted in this 1860 print drawn by Henry Cleenewerck and lithographed by R. H. Howell. The scene shows a town meeting in Johnson Square in Savannah, Georgia, as news of Abraham Lincoln's presidential election has been announced and the state has voted to secede from the Union. A banner featuring the image of a coiled rattlesnake and the words "Our Motto—Southern Rights, Equality of the States, Don't Tread on Me" is lit by celebratory fireworks and a bonfire.

Some politicians tried to make a compromise with the Southern states, allowing for slavery in the South and in new southwestern territories. But President Lincoln adamantly opposed this compromise and prepared the country for war. Lincoln's official reason for going to war was to preserve the Union, while the Southern states' reason was so that each state could make its own laws regarding slavery and not be subject to the laws made by a federal government. But both sides knew that they were really fighting over whether new territories would be slave states or free states, and they knew that the underlying reasons for war were the issues of slavery and freedom.

The Civil War

The Confederacy took hold of all but four federal forts within the Southern states that had seceded from the Union. Lincoln decided to defend these four forts that were not yet taken, one of which was Fort Sumter in South Carolina. The Confederacy demanded surrender of the fort, and when it was not surrendered, they fired upon Union forces who remained at the fort. Thus began the Civil War (1861–1865), the deadliest war in the history of the United States.

Fort Sumter was quickly lost to the Confederacy, and four more states—Virginia, Tennessee, Arkansas, and North Carolina—seceded from the Union and joined the Confederacy. The four remaining slave states—Missouri, Kentucky, Delaware, and Maryland—chose to remain loyal to the Union.

Frederick Douglass and other free slaves urged blacks to join the Union army, and many slaves escaped and ran to the Union lines seeking freedom. Still, blacks weren't initially welcomed into the Union army, and escaped slaves were actually barred from joining. It wasn't until the pool of white volunteers began to dry up and more and more men were needed to fight what was becoming a long and grueling war that the black population actually became a strong part of the Union army.

President Lincoln issued the Emancipation Proclamation on January 1, 1863, freeing all slaves in Confederate-held areas. Although it applied only to states that had seceded from the Union, the proclamation was the first step to outlawing slavery completely.

The Emancipation Proclamation said that "all persons held as slaves within any State or designated part of a State, [where] the people . . . [are] in rebellion against the United States, shall be then, thenceforward, and forever free."

It also stated that "the Executive Government of the United States, including the military and naval authority thereof, will recognize and maintain the freedom of such persons," ensuring that slaves would have their freedom under the law.

Lincoln wanted to make sure that the slaves would go free peacefully and not rise up against their former masters, so he added, "And I hereby enjoin upon the people so declared to be free to abstain from all violence, unless in necessary self-defence; and I recommend to them that, in all cases when allowed, they labor faithfully for reasonable wages."

In order to accept former slaves into the military so that they could help fight the Civil War, Lincoln stated in his Emancipation Proclamation that "such persons of suitable condition, will be received into the armed service of the United States to garrison forts, positions, stations, and other places, and to man vessels of all sorts in said service."

Both sides fought long and hard, and the war lasted for four years and claimed many lives. But finally, on April 9, 1865, Confederate general Robert E. Lee surrendered to Union general Ulysses S. Grant, and the war was over. All that was left was for both sides to pick up the pieces and move on.

Freedom

A new amendment to the Constitution—the thirteenth—was ratified in December 1865. It outlawed slavery and promised freedom to any blacks who remained enslaved. Most slave owners bowed to the new law and immediately freed their slaves. But for blacks who had no land or money and who were separated from their families, starting over was a hard thing to do.

Many stayed with their former masters, working as laborers for pay instead of as slaves. Some moved to the cities and found jobs, and others moved west to new territories. Although many were still very poor and had to work hard just to get by, often doing the same work they did as slaves, now they were their own masters. They could choose who they would work for, where they would live, and what work they would do. They could marry and be certain that their family would stay together. If they chose, they could move away, seeking work in the city or farming land in the new territories. Finally, they were free.

Still, their struggle for equality was just beginning. For years, blacks were plagued by bitter discrimination and unjust treatment. White supremacist groups like the Ku Klux Klan burned down black churches, destroyed black towns, and even murdered innocent black citizens. Others discriminated against

This 1874 Thomas Nast cartoon shows representatives from the White League and the Ku Klux Klan carrying murder weapons and shaking hands over a crest bearing symbols, including a lynched man hanging from a tree. The words at the top of the drawing are "The Union as it was. This is a white man's government. The lost cause." And finally, above the bowing black family, "Worse than slavery," showing that life after slavery was perhaps more dangerous, dehumanizing, and deadly for freed blacks than it was for slaves. Nast's message is that white lawmakers were no better for the black cause than white plantation owners had been.

blacks in the workplace and in schools. Blacks were cursed with poverty and forced to struggle for their basic needs. Even now, more than 150 years later, many black people in America still struggle to break out of the hardships and toil that slavery and the legacy of slavery brought to them.

PRIMARY SOURCE TRANSCRIPTIONS

Page 12: The U.S. Constitution

Transcription excerpt

We the people of the United States, in order to form a more perfect union, establish justice, insure domestic tranquility, provide for the common defense, promote the general welfare, and secure the blessings of liberty to ourselves and our posterity, do ordain and establish this Constitution for the United States of America.

Article I

Section 1. All legislative powers herein granted shall be vested in a Congress of the United States, which shall consist of a Senate and House of Representatives.

Section 2. The House of Representatives shall be composed of members chosen every second year by the people of the several states, and the electors in each state shall have the qualifications requisite for electors of the most numerous branch of the state legislature.

No person shall be a Representative who shall not have attained to the age of twenty five years, and been seven years a citizen of the United States, and who shall not, when elected, be an inhabitant of that state in which he shall be chosen.

Representatives and direct taxes shall be apportioned among the several states which may be included within this union, according to their respective numbers, which shall be determined by adding to the whole number of free persons, including those bound to service for a term of years, and excluding Indians not taxed, three fifths of all other Persons. The actual Enumeration shall be made within three years after the first meeting of the Congress of the United States, and within every subsequent term of ten years, in such manner as they shall by law direct. The number of Representatives shall not exceed one for every thirty thousand, but each state shall have at least one Representative; and until such enumeration shall be made, the state of New Hampshire shall be entitled to chuse three, Massachusetts eight, Rhode Island and Providence Plantations one, Connecticut five, New York six, New Jersey four, Pennsylvania eight, Delaware one, Maryland six, Virginia ten, North Carolina five, South Carolina five, and Georgia three.

Page 35: Slave Pass

Transcription

Deep Creek [??]

June 13th 1845

The bearer, Alfred Wiggins an old family servant of mine, has permission to visit my brother, William Lee Edwards, Esqr, of Fairfax County, Va, at any time during the next three months. Alfred has a sister and other relatives in Alexandria, with whom he is at liberty to spend some time also. Masters of [??] are at liberty to convey him 6 mi from the above places.

Lathorp G. Edwards

Alfred also has permission to visit Washington D.C. or any other portion of the District of Columbia, or any other place he may desire.

Wm Lee Edwards
Fairfax [??]
[??]

Page 44: Observations On the Inslaving, importing and purchasing of Negroes

Transcription
With some Advice theron, extracted from the Epistle of the Yearly-Meeting of the People called Quakers, held at London in the Year 1748.

Anthony Benezet

When ye spread forth your Hands, I will hide mine Eyes from you, yea when ye make many Prayers I will not hear; your Hands are full of Blood. Wash ye, make you clean, put away the Evil of your Doings from before mine Eyes Ifai, 1, 15.

Is not this the Feast that I have chosen, to loose the Bands of Wickedness, to undo the heavy Burden, to let the Oppressed go free, and that ye break every Yoke, Chap. 58,7.

Second Edition.
Germantown: Printed by Christopher Sower 1760.

GLOSSARY

abolitionist A person who fought to end slavery.

agility The ability to move quickly and gracefully.

ambivalent To have contradictory feelings about something or someone.

Confederacy The eleven Southern states that seceded from the Union in 1860 and 1861.

emancipate To set free or release from bondage.

fugitive A person who has fled from danger or injustice.

indentured Bound by contract into service.

plantation A large farm or estate, cultivated by workers living on it.

prejudice A judgment formed before all the facts are known.

secede To formally withdraw from membership in a political group or union.

servant A person employed to perform services for another.

slave A human being who is owned as property by another.

uprising An act of resistance or revolt.

FOR MORE INFORMATION

Harpers Ferry National Historic Park
P.O. Box 65
Harpers Ferry, WV 25425
(304) 535-6298
Web site: http://www.nps.gov/hafe

The Harriet Tubman Home
180 South Street
Auburn, NY 13021
(315) 252-2081
Web site: http://www.nyhistory.com/harriettubman/index.htm

National Underground Railroad Freedom Center
312 Elm Street
Cincinnati, OH 45202
(513) 412-6900
Web site: http://www.undergroundrailroad.org

Web Sites

Due to the changing nature of Internet links, the Rosen Publishing
Group, Inc., has developed an online list of Web sites related to the
subject of this book. This site is updated regularly. Please use this link
to access the list:

http://www.rosenlinks.com/psah/slia

 # FOR FURTHER READING

Douglass, Frederick. *Narrative of the Life of Frederick Douglass, an American Slave*. New York: Penguin Putnam Inc., 1997.

Everett, Susanne. *History of Slavery*. Greenwich, CT: Brompton Books Corp., 1991.

Hulm, David. *U.S. v. the Amistad: The Question of Slavery in a Free Country*. New York: Rosen Publishing Group, Inc., 2003.

Lindsey, Dr. Howard O. *A History of Black America*. Greenwich, CT: Brompton Books Corp., 1994.

Myers, Walter Dean. *Amistad: A Long Road to Freedom*. New York: Dutton Children's Books, 1998.

Sanders, Nancy I. *A Kid's Guide to African American History*. Chicago: Chicago Review Press, 2000.

Stowe, Harriet Beecher. *Uncle Tom's Cabin*. New York: Barnes and Noble Books, 1995.

Thomas, Velma Maia. *Lest We Forget: The Passage from Slavery to Emancipation*. New York: Crown Publishers, Inc., 1997.

BIBLIOGRAPHY

Divine, Robert A., T. H. Breen, George M. Fredrickson, R. Hal Williams, and Randy Roberts. *America, Past and Present*. Glenview, IL: Scott, Foresman and Company, 1986.

Douglass, Frederick. *Narrative of the Life of Frederick Douglass, an American Slave*. New York: Penguin Putnam Inc., 1997.

Everett, Susanne. *History of Slavery*. Greenwich, CT: Brompton Books Corp., 1991.

Kemble, Fanny, and Catherine Clinton, ed. *Fanny Kemble's Journals*. Cambridge, MA: Harvard University Press, 2000.

Kolchin, Peter. *American Slavery*. New York: Hill and Wang, 1993.

Lincoln, Abraham. Emancipation Proclamation. Retrieved February 4, 2003 (http://www.yale.edu/lawweb/avalon/emancipa.htm).

Lindsey, Dr. Howard O. *A History of Black America*. Greenwich, CT: Brompton Books Corp., 1994.

Myers, Walter Dean. *Amistad: A Long Road to Freedom*. New York: Dutton Children's Books, 1998.

Parish, Peter J. *Slavery: History and Historians*. New York: Harper and Row Publishers, 1989.

PBS. "Africans in America." Retrieved February 4, 2003 (http://www.pbs.org/wgbh/aia/part1/narrative.html).

Sanders, Nancy I. *A Kid's Guide to African American History*. Chicago: Chicago Review Press, 2000.

Stowe, Harriet Beecher. *Uncle Tom's Cabin*. New York: Barnes and Noble Books, 1995.

Thomas, Velma Maia. *Lest We Forget: The Passage from Slavery to Emancipation*. New York: Crown Publishers, Inc., 1997.

U.S. Congress. Thirteenth Amendment to the Constitution. Retrieved February 4, 2003 (http://www.law.cornell.edu/constitution/constitution.amendmentxiii.html).

White, John, and Ralph Willett. *Slavery in the American South*. New York: Harper and Row Publishers, 1970.

PRIMARY SOURCE IMAGE LIST

Page 5: Photograph of a slave family picking cotton. Photographed near Savannah, Georgia, by an American photographer circa 1860. Housed in the New-York Historical Society.

Page 10: *Landing at Jamestown, the Founding of the Colony of Jamestown, Virginia by Captain Christopher Newport and 105 of His Followers, 1607.* Lithograph created by an artist in the English school circa seventeenth century. From a private collection.

Page 12: Signed copy of the Constitution of the United States of America. 1787. Housed in the National Archives.

Page 14: Eli Whitney's patent for the cotton gin. March 14, 1794. From the records of the Patent and Trademark Office, National Archives, Washington, D.C.

Page 17: Black-and-white print of a slave caravan in Africa. Housed in the New York Public Library.

Page 18: Print depicting the death of Captain Ferrer aboard the *Amistad.* Published by John Warner Barber in New Haven, Connecticut, in 1840. Housed in the Library of Congress, Washington, D.C.

Page 19: Etching of the deck plans of the British slave ship the *Brookes.* Printed in 1789. Housed in the Library of Congress, Washington, D.C.

Page 20: Engraving of sailors throwing slaves overboard. From *Torrey's American Slave Trade,* 1822. Housed in the Library of Congress, Washington, D.C.

Page 22: Frontispiece and title page from *The Interesting Narrative of the Life of Olaudah Equiano.* Edition published in 1794. Housed in the Library of Congress, Washington, D.C.

Page 23: Print showing a slave auction in the South. Sketched by Theodore R. Davis in 1861. Printed in *Harper's Weekly.* Housed in the New York Public Library.

Page 25: *The Washington Family.* Engraving by Edward Savage, 1798. Housed in the National Portrait Gallery, Washington, D.C.

Page 28: Photograph of a group of slaves outside their quarters in Cockspur Island, Georgia. Taken in the mid-nineteenth century.

Page 30: Photographic portrait of Frederick Douglass. Taken in the 1840s.

Page 31: Portrait of Fanny Kemble Butler. Oil on canvas. Painted by Henry Inman in the nineteenth century. Housed in the Brooklyn Museum of Art, New York.

Page 33: Runaway slave broadside from November 2, 1853. Housed in the Division of Rare and Manuscript Collections at Cornell University, Ithaca, New York.

Page 35: Virginia slave pass, 1845. Housed in the Division of Rare and Manuscript Collections at Cornell University, Ithaca, New York.

Page 36: *Cruelties of Slavery* engraving from *The Anti-Slavery Record.* May 1835.

Page 38: Fugitives escaping from the eastern shore of Maryland. Wood engraving. Published in *Underground Railroad,* 1872.

Page 42: Portrait of Absalom Jones. Circa 1810. Painted by Raphaelle Peale. Housed in the Delaware Art Museum, Washington, Delaware.

Page 44: Title page from Anthony Benezet's "Observations On the Inslaving, importing and purchasing of Negroes." Second edition. Printed by Christopher Sower in 1760.

Page 46: Poster advertising *Uncle Tom's Cabin.* 1852. Color lithograph. Housed in the New-York Historical Society.

Page 47: Portrait of John Brown, 1859. Albumen silver print after a daguerreotype attributed to Martin M. Lawrence. Housed in the National Portrait Gallery, Washington, D.C.

Page 49: Lithograph *The First Flag of Independence Raised in the South, by the Citizens of Savannah, Georgia, November 8, 1860.* Drawn by Henry Cleenewerck. Lithographed by R. H. Howell, 1860. Housed in the Library of Congress, Washington, D.C.

Page 53: *The White League and the Ku Klux Klan: Worse Than Slavery,* 1874. Cartoon drawn by Thomas Nast. Engraving published in *Harper's Weekly.*

INDEX

About the Author

Tonya Buell is a freelance writer who lives in Chandler, Arizona. This is her fifth book.

Photo Credits

Cover, pp. 10, 36, 53 Private Collection/Bridgeman Art Library; title page, pp. 17, 23 Print Collection, Miriam and Ira D. Wallach Division of Art, Prints and Photographs, the New York Public Library, Astor, Lenox and Tilden Foundations; pp. 5, 46 © New-York Historical Society, New York, USA/Bridgeman Art Library; p. 12 National Archives and Records Administration, Records of the Continental and Confederation Congresses and the Constitutional Convention, 1774-1789, Record Group 360; p. 14 National Archives and Records Administration, Records of the Patent and Trademark Office, Record Group 241; p. 18 Library of Congress, General Collections; p. 19 Library of Congress, Rare Book and Special Collections Division; p. 20 Library of Congress, Washington, D.C., USA/Bridgeman Art Library; pp. 22, 38, 49 Library of Congress, Prints and Photographs Division; pp. 25, 47 © National Portrait Gallery, Smithsonian Institution/Art Resource, NY; p. 27 Hulton Archive/Getty Images; pp. 28, 44 © Corbis; p. 30 © Bettmann/Corbis; p. 31 © Brooklyn Museum of Art, New York, USA/Gift of Charles A. Schieren/Bridgeman Art Library; pp. 33, 35 © Gift of Gail '56 and Stephen Rudin, Division of Rare Books and Manuscript Collections, Cornell University Library; p. 42 Delaware Art Museum, Gift of Absalom Jones School, 1971.

Designer: Nelson Sá; Editor: Christine Poolos;
Photo Researcher: Peter Tomlinson